GW00870464

Peter Rowan is known to m[...] appearances on ITV's progr[...] and *Top Banana*. He is also [...] of the *Early Times*, human b[...] *Book of Records* and has wr[...] a number of popular children's books including the highly acclaimed *The Amazing Voyage of the Cucumber Sandwich*, which was joint winner of the 1992 Junior Science Book Prize.

He has travelled on several expeditions around the world. These include two voyages to Antarctica, when he was ship's surgeon on the research ship *Discovery*, and two treks to the jungles of Nepal. Amongst other adventures, he survived being attacked by a wild tiger and saved the life of a man trampled by a bull elephant. He's drawn on many of these experiences in this book, where he answers questions sent in to him by readers of the *Early Times*.

He is a family doctor practising in Norfolk where he lives with his wife and three children – Sarah, Edward and Joanna.

for Twins and Tess

PINCH YOUR NOSE AND TRY TO HUM

by Peter Rowan

illustrations by David Myers

KNIGHT BOOKS
Hodder and Stoughton

Printed and bound in Great Britain for Hodder and Stoughton Children's Books, a division of Hodder and Stoughton Ltd, Mill Road, Dunton Green, Sevenoaks, Kent TN13 2YA. (Editorial Office: 47 Bedford Square, London WC1B 3DP) by Cox & Wyman Ltd, Reading, Berks. Photoset by Rowland Phototypesetting Ltd, Bury St Edmunds, Suffolk.

British Library C.I.P.

A catalogue record for this book is available from the British Library

ISBN 0-340-58418-1

Contents

Chapter One
The Body in General

Dear Doctor Pete,
I've just finished reading about the Hunchback of Notre
Dame. *Have you any idea what was wrong with the poor*
man?

Quasimodo, the hunchback of Notre Dame, was a
character dreamed up by the French author Victor Hugo.
However, the descriptions of the bell ringer give some
strong clues to the condition Hugo was describing.
'. . . *a horseshoe mouth, a tiny left eye, obstructed by a*
bushy red eyebrow, while the right eye had vanished
entirely beneath an enormous wen (cyst or wart), *those*
irregular teeth notched like castle battlements, that horny
lip on which a tooth encroached like an elephant's
tusk . . .'
The body was described as '*that huge head sprouting*
between two shoulders with an enormous hump . . . *a*
system of thighs and legs so warped that they only met at
the knees, and looked, from the front, like two scythe
blades joined at the handle.'
Victor Hugo was 29 and living in Paris when he began to
write the book, in 1828, and it is highly likely that he saw or
knew of someone suffering with the medical condition
known as Von Recklinghausen's neurofibromatosis. This
condition is best known because of the so-called 'Elephant
Man' John Merrick who lived in London in the late 1800s.

It is a very rare disorder, and in its severest form, produces a person with great deformity of the bones and also of 'soft tissues' like the skin. All these are as Hugo described Quasimodo. In addition, there are often swellings of the nerves and this may cause deafness. In the book Quasimodo goes deaf – although the author says this is a result of living in the great cathedral close to the loud noise of the bells. People with the condition are often strong, agile and mentally alert despite their dreadful appearance. This is how poor Quasimodo was in the book and how the 'Elephant Man' was in real life.

Hugo must have seen someone with this condition in Paris. As great a writer as he was, even he couldn't have dreamed up such an accurate description of a real medical condition by chance. Who that poor individual was we shall never know.

This poor man's plight has often been
A butt for jokes as we have seen.
How strange it is that many find
Humour in pain of this kind!
This sad condition is for real,
Sympathy ONLY should we feel!

Dear Dr Pete,
When they used to chop people's heads off, could they still
'see' for a moment when they fell into the basket?

I suppose you have to say that nobody knows for certain. If you have your head chopped off you are no longer around to report back! It would seem to me extremely unlikely that after the blood vessels and the spinal cord were severed any meaningful messages were bouncing around between the eyes and the brain. (The part of the cerebral cortex that interprets sight is at the back of the brain under the occiput of the skull. The occiput is the part you would bang if you fell directly backwards.)

I can tell you a few stories about 'deaths' I've seen and you can make your own mind up about how long the brain remains working after death. When I worked in the heart attack unit of a busy hospital the patients were all connected up to electrical monitors. This gave us a continual reading on the state of their hearts. Quite often it was possible to see this reading suddenly come to a halt as the heart stopped because of a heart attack. The patient became unconscious almost immediately. This observation would favour the idea that a person whose head (and therefore blood supply) was cut off by an axe or guillotine would become unconscious immediately and not suffer.

Another true story happened to me when I first became a doctor and was working at the old Addenbrookes Hospital in Cambridge. A man's heart stopped during visiting time one Sunday afternoon. We restarted the man's heart and he was OK.

During Sunday visiting the Salvation Army Band used to

play in the car park outside the ward. Later on I asked the patient what he remembered about the episode. He had felt no pain and didn't remember the moment when his heart stopped. He did remember coming round as his heart started up again. His first reaction was that he was dead in heaven. The first sound he heard, even before he could see, was the sound of the Salvation Army playing hymns!

Dear Doctor Pete,
I work in a fitness centre. It appears that you can shorten your arm in the following way. Stand to attention, then put one arm out sideways until the fingers just touch a wall. Your arm should be horizontal. Then bend your arm quickly twenty times at the elbow (flexing and extending the elbow). Straighten your arm out again, and the finger tips will be several centimetres short of the wall! How is this done?

I have tried this, and yes, it appears that you can make your arm shorter. What is happening is very interesting, and relies on the great range of movement at the shoulder. The shoulder is the most mobile joint in the human body.

When you first stretch out towards the wall not only is your arm being raised but complex actions are also happening at the collarbone (clavicle) and the shoulder blade (scapula) on the back. These are all involved in shoulder movement and enable the 'reach' of the arm to be much greater than if movement was only possible at the shoulder joint itself.

Now, two of the muscles which give the shoulder joint strength and stability are the triceps and biceps. These are the muscles which you are using when you do your twenty movements at the elbow. This exercise has the result of tensing these muscles, but it also has an effect at the shoulder. When you next put your arm out straight to touch the wall these muscles have changed the position of the bones which make up the shoulder joint. In particular the shoulder-blade bone has moved further 'back' on the back.

Don't worry— bend your arm 20 times and it will fit you perfectly...

In this position, the arm appears to be shorter as not so much 'reach' is available at the shoulder. 'Reach' is very important to a boxer, who needs to land the first punch without coming within range of the opponent's fist.

Dear Doctor Pete,
Is it true that you lose five seconds of your life if you smoke a cigarette, do a false burp, or French kiss?

No. The only one of these three pastimes that shortens your life is cigarette smoking. It's been discovered by looking at statistics of the ages that people live to, and how many cigarettes some of them smoked, that men aged 35 who smoke 20 cigarettes a day have a 25% chance of dying before the age of 65. My maths isn't perfect but I make that about 328,500 cigarettes smoked if they began at 15 and died at 60. If you assume that they would have lived a normal lifetime if they hadn't smoked, that means those 328,500 smokes have cut their lives by 15 years. Divide the number of cigarettes into the 15 lost years of life and you get 24 minutes. So for those men each cigarette cost 24 minutes of life.

To produce an overall average figure that applies to all smokers is more complicated, because it depends on many factors, including exactly how many cigarettes are smoked, and luck! However I would have put the figure much higher than 5 seconds. It's much safer to stick to burping and French kissing.

Dear Dr Pete,
Is it true that when you die your life flashes before your eyes?

This is one of the many mysteries surrounding the workings of the human brain. It certainly does not happen in cases of instantaneous death. It may in circumstances where death comes slowly with suffocation of one kind or another, such as drowning or hanging.

One theory is that, as the brain is starved of oxygen – as in drowning – the areas within it that store memory go absolutely berserk, and fire off a confused series of images from the past. Quite why these areas are particularly sensitive to lack of oxygen, or indeed exactly where they are, is uncertain. However other parts of the brain – the cerebral cortex – stay 'conscious' long enough to appreciate this sudden flood of information from the past.

There is no doubt that this phenomenon happens, as many people who have been saved at the last moment have described their life flashing backwards through their mind at great speed and with great clarity.

Dear Dr Pete,
Is the body the same temperature all over?

The answer is no. The 'normal' temperature of the human body taken in the mouth varies between about 36 and 37.2 degrees Centigrade. There is usually an arrow at 37°C on home thermometers that parents (and doctors) use to mark the middle of this range. So normal body temperature varies a great deal. It tends to be lower in the morning than at night. It's lowest in the early hours of the morning while you are asleep. (As a matter of interest the domestic goat has the highest normal body temperature of any mammal – about 39.9°C.)

The reading also varies according to where you put the thermometer. Under the tongue is the usual place, but when doctors take small babies' temperatures (and older children who might bite the glass thermometer) they either put it under an arm or in the rectum (backpassage). The temperature under the arm is lower than the rectal temperature, which is getting closer to measuring the hotter inner core of the body.

So not all parts of the body are at the same temperature. The temperature of the hands and feet is colder than the inner trunk. This is most noticeable on a cold day when the outside air cools the blood as it runs into the extremities. Blood leaving the trunk to run down the leg is at about 35°C. It cools as it travels down to the foot. When it arrives at the big toe it is probably at room temperature.

This cooling is not just the result of heat loss into the air. In fact, not a lot of heat is lost this way. The human body has a very clever heat exchange mechanism to manage body heat in the four limbs. In particular it has a way to prevent cold blood from the feet arriving back at the heart. Cold blood returning to the heart could cause damage. Without this arrangement it could be dangerous to walk in snow!

Arteries taking warm blood to the feet are surrounded by conveniently-placed veins taking blood away from the feet. This cooler blood is thus warmed up very nicely, and heat is saved. By the time the blood from the feet enters the trunk in the groin area it is nearly back to 37°C.

The hottest part of the body is probably the area of brain set deep (about 5 cm) behind the spot on the face between the eyes. The reason is that the head – the brain in fact – receives for its size by far the greatest proportion of the blood output of the heart. The brain needs a continuous high blood flow to work well. As you sit reading this your brain is taking nearly 16%* of this blood supply. This blood straight from the heart is warm and hence the temperature inside the skull is as hot as the normal body gets. (It may only take 8 seconds for a blood cell to leave the heart, go around the brain, and get back to the heart! A journey to the big toe may take nearly 60 seconds.) The chest is not as hot as you might expect because slightly cooler blood is returning from the outermost parts of the body, and cooler air is also being drawn into the lungs by breathing.

Special cameras which show pictures of the body taken using heat rather than light have shown this to be true.

*The heart pumps about 5 litres of blood out per minute, and 800 millilitres of this goes to the brain.

Chapter Two
Mind and Emotions

Dear Dr Pete,
Please answer the following question. Why do you go pale if you are frightened, and blush red if you are embarrassed?

The reason is the movement of blood in the skin. If you are frightened hormones, such as adrenaline, are released into the bloodstream by two glands in the abdomen on top of the kidneys. These hormones are often called the 'fight or flight' hormones since they prepare the body for whatever may be causing the fright.

They move blood to the muscles so that more oxygen is available for either fighting or running away. That blood has to come from somewhere, and the skin is ideal. Small blood vessels in the skin narrow to move the blood flow away and the skin looks pale.

As a matter of interest, blood is also pulled away from the intestines for the emergency. This slows down digestion and can make the body sick. (This also happens during exercise and is the reason you are often warned not to run around and exercise after a big meal.)

When you are embarrassed something else occurs – since being embarrassed is not exactly the same thing as being frightened. (Some experts think that embarrassment can be thought of as a very mild fright.)

Again adrenaline is behind what happens. It causes blood vessels to widen in certain areas of the skin. These are often ones on the face. When the blood vessels widen, more blood flows in and there's your blush. It all happens very fast and there is not a lot you can do to stop it!

Dear Dr Pete,
Is it true that if you listen to something while you sleep, you remember it when you wake up in the morning.

No. Sadly this is not true. It would make swotting for exams easier if it were.

There are two types of memory, short-term and long-term, and the names explain what they are. For long-term memory to take place, permanent changes must take place in the brain cells and their connecting pathways. These are probably chemical changes. Not all short-term memory, which is probably messages travelling around the brain along certain pathways, is converted to long-term memory.

Let's say you wanted to learn a poem by heart and you recorded it on tape and arranged for it to play repeatedly overnight. During sleep the parts of the brain concerned with memory are being rested and will not take in the information and store it.

In fact, sleep is an important time when the body can relax and recover ready for the next day. If you lose sleep your memory will not be so good the next day, although it will soon recover. So if you are working hard for exams it's important to sleep well and not stay up doing last minute cramming.

Dear Doctor Pete,
Is it true that people dying of thirst in the desert see mirages?

There are two different ways that someone in the desert could imagine that water is present when it is not. The first is if that person is really ill, because of lack of water. In this dehydrated state he or she could become confused and 'see' imaginary water.

The second way involves an optical illusion and can be experienced by any normal healthy person. The usual sighting is of a sheet of water in the hot desert or on a hot road.

These mirages can form in various ways, and all rely on the bending of light rays. Usually light rays reach our eyes in straight lines. However if light rays pass through two layers of air with different densities then they may be bent. Layers of air may have different densities if they are, for some reason due to local atmospheric conditions, at different temperatures.

The common mirage in the desert is caused by the hot sand heating the air up immediately above it. This hotter air close to the sand is less dense than the air above it. Where these two layers of air meet they can act like a mirror, and reflect light on to the eye from distant objects. Images of the sky may be seen – apparently on the sand. This can look like a patch of water – especially if you are thirsty and longing to find water.

You can see this yourself on a hot day on the road. Crouch down close to a hot tarmac road – NOT when there are cars coming! – and you may see what looks like a shining sheet of water. It is in fact an image of the sky.

Dear Dr Pete,
Why do people bite their lip when in pain? Surely that causes more pain?

Pain is one of the most mysterious of the senses. As well as pain your skin has special receptors for cold, warmth, touch and pressure. When these are 'triggered' a message in a nerve travels to the spinal cord, and then up to the brain.

The message is received in a relay station called the thalamus. This part of the brain then sends the signal on to the cerebral cortex. This is the 'thinking' part of the brain. If any action is required – perhaps the bath water is too hot – then the cortex can instruct the muscles of the hand to turn on the cold tap. (If the water was really hot then fast action can be taken at spinal cord level to save time. A reflex movement will quickly pull the hand out of the water.)

However, pain control is far more complex than this simple model. At various places the pain sensation may be modified. Natural painkillers called endorphins can be released to 'kill' the pain. This is one theory for how acupuncture works – the technique causes these endorphins to be released.

If the pain message gets past these chemicals it can still be halted in the brain. The system which can do this seems to operate if the brain concentrates on something else. So biting your lip may distract your mind from an incoming pain signal. The same sort of thing goes on in the heat of battle or on the playing field. If the body is busy with an important activity, like fighting or playing a game, pain may not be felt until afterwards. So the football player does not realise that he or she has been kicked hard on the shin until the final whistle.

The system works the other way round too. If someone warns you that some pain is coming the expectation of it can make the whole experience much more painful. For some people this form of pain anticipation is often involved in visits to the dentist.

Dear Doctor Pete,
Recently I read Edgar Allan Poe's story 'The mysterious case of Mr M Valdemir' in which, during his moment of death, the man in question was hypnotised and was kept alive by the hypnotist. Would it, in real life, be possible for the moment of death to be prolonged by hypnosis?

No. Hypnotism is a state of extreme suggestion. Hypnotists are not able to 'suggest' impossible ideas to people. A hypnotist can not fly in the face of death. If they could they would be very popular in hospital intensive care units.

Nor are hypnotists able to suggest things that their subjects do not truly wish for. This is why the success rate of 'suggesting' that a smoker stops smoking is not very high. Deep down the smoker may wish to continue.

There are states of very deep relaxation which are similar to what is popularly called hypnosis. Indian fakirs (wise religious men) are often shown in this state of meditation. The pulse slows and these people look to be in a state of suspended animation; but they can not cheat death in this way.

Dear Doctor Pete,
Is there such a thing as keeping a stiff upper lip when you are sad?

This is a command, often associated with soldiers, which means be brave and do not show your emotions. All of us feel sad at some time or another, and crying is one way of showing distress. Some people, often men, feel that showing distress in this way is a sign of weakness.

If you do try and suppress your emotions there may still be some giveaway signs. The body may shake and breathing can be interrupted by sobs. Even if you do manage to suppress these signs, one part of body language that is very hard to hide is when the upper lip starts to quiver. Hence the command 'keep a stiff upper lip'.

Dear Doctor Pete,
What is happening to the body when you feel 'butterflies'
in the stomach?

This is a feeling that comes as the body prepares for some kind of action – often associated with being tense or frightened. Let's say you are going to be summoned to the head teacher at school and you know you are in trouble. The brain prepares the body for this just as if you were living in a cave 20,000 years ago and were being chased by a wild animal. Blood is automatically diverted to important areas like the brain and the muscles. It carries the oxygen to give the energy which may be needed for fight or flight. (A chemical messenger called adrenaline is involved in this – it's often called the 'fight or flight' hormone. See p. 18).

As the blood is quickly diverted away from areas like the skin and the stomach, where it is not needed in the emergency, you may notice several changes in your body. The skin goes white, and there is a feeling in the stomach, very well described as a fluttering of butterflies, as the blood suddenly surges away.

Dear Dr Pete,
Can you tell me what stage fright is? Is there a cure for it? I have suddenly developed it and it is affecting drama which I really enjoy. When I get it my hands won't stop shaking. So please HELP!

He decided to remove them because they were chattering so much...

Stage fright is a feeling of fear. When you are frightened of something – in your case appearing in front of people on the stage – a chemical called adrenaline is released into the blood. This has a number of effects, including shaky hands, increased sweating, and a thumping fast heart. All this is designed to get you ready for action. But the feeling itself upsets a lot of people.

The way around this is to adopt a positive attitude to the first surge of adrenaline, and to be ready for it. After all, it is a natural thing to happen. Here are some tips to fight any form of anxiety – which is what this is.

1. Sit down somewhere quiet when you begin to feel anxious. Or better still, lie down in your bedroom and close your eyes.

2. Breathe in slowly and deeply. Hold your breath in for a second and then breathe out even more slowly. Do this for 5 to 10 minutes.

3. Clench your hands while you breathe in, and relax them as you breathe out. It also helps to talk to friends about how you feel. When you realise what is happening, the feeling will often go.

Don't be too hard on yourself. It's not easy when you first go on the stage. When I was first on a live TV show, I was sweating so much that I thought I'd borrow an anti-perspirant to spray under my arms. I was in such a state that I accidentally sprayed on some starch which was lying around the dressing room! But I survived.

Chapter Three
Brain, Nerves and the Five Senses

Dear Doctor Pete,
Can you test how fast someone thinks by dropping a ruler
and asking them to catch it?

Yes. You can test a person's reactions by holding a ruler at one end and dangling the other end between their thumb and first finger. Ask them to catch it when you let go. Their fingers should be about 2 cm apart and they must not know when you are going to drop it.

Reflexes tend to slow up as you get older so your reaction time is certainly faster than your grandparents' and probably faster than your parents'.

This'll get your measure!

One experiment you can do if you find an adult who has been drinking alcohol is to test their reaction time, and then re-test them later when they haven't had a drink. They might be surprised how much an alcoholic drink can slow them down. This is one reason why driving cars and drinking are so dangerous and do not mix.

Dear Dr Pete,
What are pins and needles and how are they caused?

'Pins and Needles' is a familiar sensation to most people, and the cause is some sort of interruption to the normal working of a nerve. There are lots of causes which can give this feeling – a sensation which is a mixture of numbness and a feeling that pins are being jabbed into the skin.

One common cause is sleeping awkwardly, so that a nerve in an arm or leg gets squashed by your sleeping body weight. When you wake up the blood begins to flow freely again, and as the nerve to the arm starts to work fully there is a short period of altered sensation. This is pins and needles.

As I say, there is more than one cause. The spinal cord is contained within the vertebral bones of the back. A 'slipped disc' is a condition when the cartilage forming a 'disc' between each of the bones of the spine (vertebrae) 'slips' and pushes on one of the nerves running out of the spinal cord. This will give either a numb feeling or 'pins and needles' in the area that particular nerve is running to. So if it is a nerve to the foot, you will feel the problem in the foot, although the trouble is in fact between the spinal bones of the lower back.

Dear Dr Pete,
I read a Roald Dahl story about a man whose brain and one eye were kept alive after he died. Is this possible?

Yes, I think it is. The story is called *William and Mary* and I have reread it to check if everything that Mr Dahl says happens to William's brain would be possible.

Without giving the ending of the story away, a neurosurgeon waits at the bedside of his friend William who is dying from a stomach cancer. When this cancer eventually kills the man, the neurosurgeon immediately hitches up William's healthy brain to an artificial blood supply. (Mr Dahl uses all the correct terms and his knowledge of the anatomy of the brain is perfect.)

The surgeon then removes the brain and its protective cover – the dura – from the skull. He leaves just one input of information to this brain – an eye and its nerve.

I have talked to one of my friends who is a neurologist and, like me, he thinks this would be technically very very difficult, but NOT impossible. The spinal cord is cut but this would leave memory and all the so-called higher thinking processes of the brain intact and working – as long as it continued to be fed by the artificial heart, pumping the artificial blood with its nutrients and oxygen.

In the book, the brain is prevented from drying out by being continually bathed in a fluid. It would also be important not to let the brain become infected. It would be very vulnerable without the skull and skin to protect it.

No one – as far as I know – has ever had both the necessary skill and the urge to do this! But in theory I think it must be possible.

Dear Dr Pete,
Do footballers ever get injured from heading the ball?

Very rarely, because they 'head' with the front of the head and brace the neck muscles at the back of the head for the impact. Also, footballs are not rock hard and will not break the skull's bones under normal circumstances.

There is one part of the skull which is especially vulnerable to blows to the head in sport – the side of the head in the temporal region. That's the area roughly above and slightly in front of the ear. There is an artery under the skull here which can very easily be snapped by an apparently minor blow from something such as a golf ball, a cricket ball, or even a football. This is why cricket helmets have special protection for the temple and side of the head.

Always report it if someone is knocked out, especially if the blow is to the side of the head, and even if they seem initially to recover quickly.

Dear Dr Pete,
I heard once of a dancer who had got a sort of numbness in her feet so that if she cut her feet she couldn't feel any pain at all. Of course this was dangerous as if she was bleeding to death she wouldn't know. Is this numbness actually possible, and if so how does it happen?

There is no condition I know about in which dancing or marching causes numbness in the feet.

However, there are conditions of the nervous system which give rise to numb feet. Dancers can get these just as anyone else can.

1. Some people are born insensitive to pain. They may feel heat, cold, vibration, and be able to see, smell, taste and hear, but they just do not recognise pain. This, of course, can cause great problems, as parts of their body may become damaged because there is no early warning 'pain' signal.

2. There is an uncommon condition in which sensation in the feet is altered so that the sufferer feels numbness. This can happen in the hands too. The area affected is usually said to be 'glove and stocking' because the skin involved would be the area covered by gloves and stockings. There are lots of causes for this, and in some rare cases patients are simply born with the condition. (This is known as Charcot-Marie-Tooth Disease.*)

The only way I know of that dancers (and skaters) can alter the nervous system is when they spin repeatedly. This affects the balance ('vestibular reflex') mechanism in the inner ear, which is lost; these people do not get dizzy when they get off a roundabout!

*named after the three doctors who first described this rare condition.
Jean Charcot, French Neurologist, 1825–1893
Pierre Marie, French Neurologist, 1853–1940
Howard Tooth, British Physician, 1856–1925

Dear Dr Pete,
Why do we itch, and why do we scratch itches?

An 'itch' is a sensation. There are others, such as pain, touch, heat, and cold. Each of these last four has its own nerves to carry the message to the brain. An 'itch' probably is carried in the pain nerve fibres. As yet, scientists are not absolutely certain about this.

Mild stimulation of pain nerve fibres produces the feeling of itching. If these fibres are stimulated *more* – perhaps by scratching the skin harder rather than tickling it with a feather – then the brain registers that as pain, and not an itch. That's why we scratch an itch. Scratching overwhelms the sensation of itching with a more powerful one.

There are still many things to learn about itching. No-one knows why an itch can begin without any stimulation to the skin. Many people start scratching if they see someone else scratching. Their brain somehow translates something that they are seeing into something they feel. I wonder how many of you have started scratching while you read this?

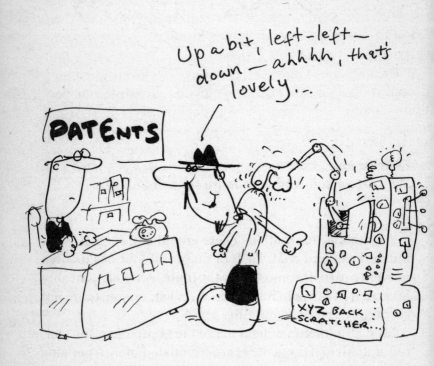

Dear Doctor Pete,
If there is blood in your tongue why can't you taste it?

Blood does have a distinctive taste. Most people have cut themselves at some time or other and know this. However, it must come into contact with the taste buds on the surface of the tongue for this to happen. If the blood is actually inside the tongue itself, then it is contained within blood vessels and does not register the 'taste' sensation to these taste buds outside.

Any taste has to be dissolved in spit (saliva) before the taste buds can identify it. These buds in fact are not just on the top of the tongue, but also on the roof of the mouth (palate) and at the back of the throat. You have about 9,000 of them! Some of these will disappear as you grow up, and you won't be able to taste sweet things as easily when you are older.

Just as there are three primary colours (red, blue and green) there are four primary tastes. These are sweet, bitter, sour and salt. Most of the sweet taste buds are on the tip of the tongue, most of the bitter ones towards the back.

Dear Dr Pete,
Can you please answer these questions about eyes:

1. *Why do things look red when you close your eyes and look at the sun?*

Bright sunlight can easily shine through your eyelids. Eyelids have blood vessels in them, and as blood is red, things look red – not black.

Don't look directly at such a bright source of light such as the sun. The light rays can damage the back of the eye. When Galileo was perfecting the first telescope he looked at the sun through it and went partially blind as a result.

2. *I've got an old teddy bear, and when I kiss her her eyes look crossed. Why?*

The human eye has a great depth of field. That means you can focus from the horizon down to this book without any problem. Many animals don't have this great range. Deer, for example, have a very good sense of smell and hearing, but their eyesight is not as good as ours.

Our two eyes are about 6 cm apart. Each one gives the brain a slightly different viewpoint. The result of this is three dimensional vision.

However there is a limit to how close our two eyes can work. When you kiss your teddy bear you are so close that three dimensional binocular vision fails. The result is an optical illusion that the bear's eyes are crossed. (Humans have not developed eyes that can see that close, probably because there is no practical advantage to such a system.)

3. *Why can't you see things well in the dark if you look directly at them?*

The back (retina) of the eye has two sorts of light-sensitive cells. These are called rods and cones. Cones detect colour and rods detect brightness of light. The rods tend to be situated around the edge of the retina, and the cones in the centre. In daylight, this works well since we use the centre of the retina the most – and the brain gets the best colour picture.

However, in the dark the rods work much better. So your peripheral vision comes into its own. Experiment with this in bed tonight when the lights are out. Look directly at something and you'll find it may almost vanish. Although if you look to one side of it, it will appear in your 'side' vision. As a matter of interest, chickens have no rods in their eyes and are blind at night.

4. *Why do eyes sometimes look red in photographs?*

When the flashlight of a camera is close to the lens, its light may bounce straight back from the retina of the eye on to the film. The retina is red because of its blood vessels. These make for the red effect in the picture. The camera has taken a picture of the back of the eye. Some modern cameras have a device to eliminate this. Before the main flash goes off to take the picture, they give a small initial flash. This first flash of light causes the subject's pupils to constrict, and prevents the light bouncing back from the retina through the lens on to the film. Another way to eliminate this 'red eye' effect if your flash is not built into the camera is to move the flash slightly away from the camera.

Dear Doctor Pete,
Why does my voice sound different when recorded on tape?

On a tape recording you hear how your voice sounds to the rest of the world. When you speak you hear your own voice from inside your skull. The sound travels through your bones and other tissues to your brain. This gives it a different quality to the sound of your voice travelling through air to someone else's ears.

No one else will ever hear your voice as you do. And the only way you can hear how you sound to others is to listen to a recording.

Dear Doctor Pete,
When it's dark – or if we have our eyes closed – how is it
possible to know exactly where a sound is coming from?

By having two ears. The brain can compare the signals coming from each ear and work out to within three degrees the origin of the sound. Owls are even better at this, and can locate sounds to within one degree. This is because they have a slightly different ear arrangement. One ear is set slightly further forward than the other.

Dear Doctor Pete,
Is it possible to smell under water?

In theory, yes. But it's difficult to do without drowning! Particles of any smell dissolve in the watery covering of the inside of the roof of the nose. Special cells then send the smell signals to the brain. Some fish can smell. That's one way sharks find their food in water.

Not all creatures smell with noses like us. Snakes smell with their tongues. Bees seem to smell with the last eight joints of their legs. Even snails smell. You can test this in the summer with a piece of lettuce. Put the lettuce in a glass bottle and the snail will slide straight by. Leave the lettuce out in the open and the snail will head straight for it. Try it and see.

It's interesting to ask people what their favourite smell is. You could do a survey in your class. Most people will go for food or drink. This shows the real purpose of smell for animals – to guide us towards things to eat and drink.

Smells are very interesting. Most people can only distinguish between about 4,000 smells. But it is possible to train your nose to tell up to 10,000. People whose job it is to test wines learn how to do this. The sense of smell is the one of our five senses which humans have allowed to fall into disuse. It's a pity. Did you know that female gorillas smell like India rubber? Or that the 'fresh' smell of the ground after a shower is due to the release of tiny fungus spores?

Dear Dr Pete,
Which part of the body is best for testing the temperature of bath water?

The choice seems to be between the toes, the hand and the elbow. These are all ideal because you get an idea of water temperature and you can pull out quickly if the water is too hot or too cold. The head is obviously an impractical body part to dip into very hot water.

Now, which part of the hand, the foot and the elbow is the most ideal heat detector? Mothers bathing babies tend to favour the elbow, and I would agree with them. The foot is as far away from the centre of the body as you can get. This means it is significantly cooler than the core body temperature of 37°C (see p. 15). So a foot might tend to 'read' the bath water as hotter than it really is in relation to 37°C.

The hand might be better than the foot, but again its temperature is very variable (warmer than a foot), and is not as reliable as an elbow. (The back of the hand has many more heat sensors than cold sensors. For every one cold sensor there are 6 heat ones.)

I like the elbow because the skin is of average thickness, the temperature is more constant than the feet and hands, and also important, there is little fat under the skin.

Fat under the skin tends to insulate the body from temperature changes, and would give insensitive readings of water temperature. For this reason the buttocks are definitely not suitable for being dipped into the water first – even if this was an easy thing to do!

Note. Skin contains four basic types of sensors. These nerve endings register hot, cold, pain and touch. A lot of sensations are a mixture of information. So, for example, kissing is a mixture of heat and touch.

Chapter 4
Muscles, Bones, Joints, Cartilage, Ligaments, Tendons and Movement

Dear Dr Pete,
You said on the radio that men and women both have the same number of ribs. Is this true?

Yes, it is usually true. I think a lot of people get confused about this because in the Bible it says that God took a rib from Adam and made Eve. There is also an odd fact about the human body which might cause confusion.

Normally men and women do have 12 ribs each. That's 12 on each side of the body. You can feel them at the front and back of your own chest. Most of us are familiar with these from pictures of skeletons.

However many people do have an extra rib. When it occurs it's in the lower neck near the collar bone. Some books say as many as one person in twenty has one. (My anatomy books put it much lower at 0.5%. That's one in 200.) Anyway, it's probably somewhere between the two. Many people have one and never know because it doesn't ever bother them.

However, and this is the important part as far as this question goes, men seem to have an extra rib more often than women. It might be as much as three times more often. So in days past when people read the Bible, and perhaps saw male skeletons with extra ribs on gallows and gibbets, they might have assumed falsely that all men have one more rib than women.

Dear Dr Pete,
Why does my head bounce off the pillow when I sneeze?

When you sneeze all sorts of muscles contract (shorten) quickly so that the air of the sneeze shoots out of your nose at the speed of a hurricane. This blows away anything irritating the lining of the nose. Some of these muscles also have the effect of pulling the head forward. You notice this more when you are lying down than when you sneeze standing up. There are lots of muscles that you have no control over when you sneeze. Try sneezing with your eyes open next time. You won't be able to! The eye muscles will shut your eyes for a fraction during the sneeze.

Dear Dr Pete,
Why do boys' Adam's apples stick out more than girls'? Is this one way of telling male and female skeletons apart?

The Adam's apple is made of cartilage. Cartilage is a tough, smooth tissue often called gristle. There are various forms, but they are not part of the bone of the skeleton. So, for example, if a scientist – or a policeman – wanted to know if a skeleton dug up is of a male or a female, the cartilage will have disappeared and will not be of any help. I've listed the main differences between male and female skeletons below.

'Adam's apple' is part of the larynx. Several cartilages make up this 'voice box' at the front of the throat. A tube –

Adam's apple is cartilage
Not bone as some do allege.
So skeletons can sometimes be
Mistaken for 'she' instead of 'he'!!

DIG...

the trachea – connects this structure to the lungs below in the chest.

The largest of the cartilages is called the thyroid cartilage. It is shaped like a snow plough and it is the front of this 'snow plough' that's called the 'Adam's apple'. It usually sticks out more in boys than in girls.

Your voice is produced in the larynx. This is not however its only job. The larynx provides an airway into the lungs, and it has a trapdoor made of cartilage (the epiglottis) at the top end that protects the lungs from food 'going the wrong way'. If food meant for the stomach should get past this barrier, you may choke.

The 'Adam's apple' gets its name from the idea that the forbidden fruit in the Garden of Eden stuck in Adam's throat.

In general, male skeletons tend to be rougher, coarser, and have more lumps and bumps than females. The reason is that males have stronger muscles and the 'lumps and bumps' are where tendons attach these muscles to bones.

The other big difference is in the pelvis. If you look down on the female pelvis it is more oval or rounded than the male, which tends to be heart-shaped. There are no bony projections into the pelvic space on the female. The reason for this is that when a woman gives birth, the baby's head – the largest part – must travel down through the pelvis and not get stuck.

Given a complete skeleton an expert could sex it nine times out of ten. It is helpful if the expert knows which race it is, because there tend to be racial differences between skeletons. Male Asian skeletons, for example, tend to be quite slight in comparison to many other males, and could be mistaken for females of another race.

Dear Dr Pete,
Do growing pains really exist?

Yes. When young people are growing quickly the growth of the long bones, of the arms and legs, can outstrip the tendons which attach these muscles to the bones. This can cause pain where the tendons are inserted into the bone, and may continue until tendon growth catches up. These are usually called growing pains, and are not serious.

Dear Dr Pete,
How do ballet dancers manage to stand on their toes?

(I asked Isabella Bambridge (13) of the Royal Ballet School, London about this, since I am not a ballet dancer myself!)

Ballet dancers wear shoes with hard square ends and strong backs (soles). These are called 'points'. Even with training a ballet dancer can not stand on his or her toes in bare feet.

In addition to these special shoes, the ballet dancer trains and develops strong ankles and a good sense of balance. Toe nails are kept cut short to guard against ingrowing toe nails.

So that's all there is to it – and a lot of practice.

Dear Dr Pete,
How can some people wiggle their ears, and flare their nostrils?

All of us have three small muscles around each ear. These attach the ear to the skull and scalp. Some animals move their ears to pick up the direction of a sound. You often see a dog 'prick up' its ears like this. The part of the human ear outside the head doesn't really need to act like a satellite dish any more. We don't have to hunt for food or look out for animals as our ancestors used to do millions of years ago.

I'm told he can wiggle his ears very fast...

However, some people can still move these muscles to wiggle their ears. (I am told Napoleon's second wife, Marie Louise, could not only wiggle her ears, but also turn them inside out!)

Now the nose! There are four small muscles (on each side) which some people can move. Again these are hardly necessary for humans, who do not need to be able to smell an enemy or some food coming.

The muscle which flares the nostril is called Dilator naris. It is helped by a muscle called Depressor septi.

The other two muscles are called Procerus and Compressor naris. Procerus runs from between the eyebrows to the upper part of the bridge of the nose. Compressor naris runs down from the bridge of the nose to the bone of the face near the upper incisor – the 'eye' tooth.

There are many other muscles that move the face. Most of them are bigger and stronger than these four muscles. That's why you must not move your mouth when you attempt to see if you can truly move your nose.

The ability to use these muscles tends to run in families. This is obvious when you think about it. Brothers and sisters often have similar smiles and expressions.

Dear Dr Pete,
What is a 'funny' bone?

The 'funny' bone is the area on the inner side of the elbow joint. It is here that a nerve called the ulnar nerve passes over the bone of the ulna, and close to the skin. You can feel the nerve in a notch in the ulna bone. Bend your elbow slightly and the notch is easily felt on the lower, inner part of the elbow.

The lower part of the elbow is obviously a place where the nerve, running close to the skin, is vulnerable to a knock against the bone. When this happens the strange 'electric shock' feeling is produced that we all call the 'funny bone'. It should really be called a 'funny nerve'.

As a matter of interest, the long bone above the elbow which runs to the shoulder is called the humerus. The words 'funny', 'humerus' and 'humorous' are merely co-incidence.

Dear Dr Pete,
What's your Achilles heel?

This is the tendon at the back of the leg which connects the muscles of the calf with the bones of the heel. The best way to feel it in action is to stand on your toes.

The achilles tendon (tendo calcaneus) is the thickest and strongest tendon or sinew in the human body. It's about 15 cm long and begins around the middle of the back of the calf. It gradually narrows and thickens down towards the back of the ankle where it is fixed to the calcaneus bone (the big one under the back of the foot). It enables the

muscles of the calf to work at the ankle joint and give the propelling force needed for walking, running and leaping. It's often sprained by athletes and if this happens the body is greatly incapacitated.

The legend of the Achilles heel comes from the Greek tale of how Achilles's mum Thetis took her son down to the magic river Styx. She dipped him in the river because she believed the water would make him invulnerable. Sadly for him she held on to him by one heel when she did this. So the heel stayed dry and remained his one weak spot. He was eventually killed by a poisoned arrow which hit him in this heel area. The saying has come to mean any vulnerable spot in a person's character.

Dear Dr Pete,
What exactly is the biggest muscle in the human body?

In an article a few weeks ago I said the answer was Gluteus Maximus – the buttock or bottom muscle. I've since had a letter arguing that the answer might be the uterus (womb). It's an interesting point. First of all I have to say that in 50% of the population (men) gluteus maximus definitely is the biggest.

The uterus, in case you do not know, is a hollow muscle that females have in their pelvis. When the body is not pregnant the uterus is about the size of a duck's egg. In this state it weighs about 30 grammes. During the nine months of pregnancy it increases in size dramatically to about 1 kg.

The gluteus maximus, on the other hand, is a sheet of muscle which moves the hip joint, and it's the one which all the medical books – and the Guinness Book of Records – give as the biggest in the body. In fact, now I've thought about it, I doubt if gluteus maximus does weigh 1kg. However record books tend to consider parts of the body in the usual state. So I don't think they'd consider the uterus, firstly because it's only 1 kg in the latter part of pregnancy, and secondly because half of us haven't got one!

The longest muscle in the human body is the sartorius. This runs like a thin ribbon at the front of the thigh from the pelvis to the top of the shin bone. It bends the hip and knee joint as when sitting cross-legged like a tailor. (The name comes from a Latin word meaning tailor). The strongest muscle in the body for its size is probably the masseter muscle which closes the mouth and clenches the jaw.

The muscle with the longest name in the body is certainly levator labii superioris aloeque nasi. It runs from the inner corner of the eye to the nostril.

So I think you have to decide for yourself which is the biggest muscle in the body. There are all sorts of ways of measuring 'biggest' or 'greatest'. If you went by length it would be sartorius. Gluteus maximus and the uterus wouldn't get a look in.

I sent this article to the *Guinness Book of Records* to see what they said. In fact, I began to work for the *Guinness Book of Records* as a result of this letter, and the uterus does now get a mention!

Generally this Record book is not very kind to off-beat entries. A few years ago I went fishing down near the South

Pole. For a bit of fun I measured how long my line went out from my rod and reel. (There's not a lot else to do down there!) I have this on a certificate signed by witnesses including the Captain of my ship *Discovery*. *Discovery* is a scientific ship and is very accurate at measuring these sorts of things. My line, with its hook on one end and me on the other, was out 913.5 yards (845.09 metres). The Guinness Book of Records refused to accept this as a record when I sent it to them because they said I hadn't caught anything!

Dear Dr Pete,
When we run for a long time, how do we get 'stitches', and what makes them painful?

The sharp pain in the side of the body that's called a stitch is a form of cramp. Cramp is a pain felt when the muscle goes into a spasm. On a long run, muscles that may not be used to hard work – perhaps because the body is unfit – may go into such spasms. This is a cramp.

There is a large flat muscle between the belly and the chest which works the breathing action of the lungs. This muscle, and the smaller ones between the ribs, may develop a cramp when you go for a long run as they have to work harder to breathe and bring more oxygen into the body. As these muscles work the rib cage like a bellows you feel this form of cramp as a sharp pain in the side.

Don't let it worry you. but you may find you get an extra stitch when you run.

If you stop running and bend forward the pain will usually go quickly. This is firstly because you have rested the muscles, and secondly because stretching a muscle with cramp will tend to relieve the spasm.

There is a plant called stitchwort which grows wild in the hedgerows. People once thought that it cured a stitch.

Dear Dr Pete,
Would you please explain how when you bend one finger of the hands, the other fingers also bend at the same time? It would be interesting to know about this.

This is a very interesting question. For the answer to what happens in the hands, it is best to start by looking at what happens in the feet. Human beings are not able to move individual toes. The action of curling the toes is called flexing (the opposite movement is called extending) and I bet you can't curl just one toe and leave the rest out straight. The muscles working the tendons that pull on the bones of the toes do not run exclusively to just one toe. Contract one muscle and all the toes will move. (We have quite limited fine control over our feet. Monkeys can grasp branches with their feet, and use them for quite delicate actions. Our feet are mainly used for walking.)

Now the hands are not quite the same. Humans are able to do much finer work with their hands than with their toes. I mean, it's easier to pick up a cup or a biscuit using your hands than your feet.

And it's between the thumb and index finger that this fine movement is seen at its best. The thumb is set at right angles to the other fingers, and can move easily to the other four fingers to pick things up. (Try picking something up using your fingers but not your thumb.) Because it's next to the thumb and is the one used most for this kind of work, the index finger has its own exclusive muscle so that it is able to move independently of the other fingers. This has not evolved – yet – in the rest of the hand. There are very often shared muscles between the fourth (ring) and fifth (little) finger in particular. In practice this links them together. It means, for example, that you will probably not be able to touch your palm with your little finger without the fourth finger coming along for the ride!

The working of the hand is something that makes humans much more advanced than other animals*. We have developed the hand as a very special tool that can lift a suitcase, play a piano or write a letter. And, of course, there are very many other varied actions that the hands are capable of.

Have a look at your hands now and you can understand how their design makes all this possible. Much of the power to work your fingers comes from muscles up in the arm. Wiggle your fingers and watch the long tendons on the back of your hand move. These strong tendons allow the arm muscles to work the fingers from a distance. This enables your fingers to be both slim and strong. If the muscles were in the hand itself it would be a very chunky part of the body which would find fine, delicate work quite difficult.

The contents of the hand are quite surprising. Each hand has twenty-seven bones. The wrist alone has eight. They can all slide over one another to give great flexibility as the hand is manoeuvred exactly into place. As this happens each finger has an unbelievable thirty muscles moving it!

Hands are still improving. In thousands of years human beings will probably be able to move all the fingers of each hand completely independently. As things are now, though, most of us have to settle for just our index (first) finger being able to do this.

*The other two things which place us apart from animals are speech, and the relatively large cerebral cortex of the brain which can think, reason, and then using the power of speech, discuss new ideas with others.

Dear Dr Pete,
I saw you at the Guinness Exhibition with the world's
tallest man. Why did you measure his feet?

Because at 14½ inches (37cms) long he has the biggest feet in the world, and he wanted to get into the *Guinness Book of Records*. (Without his size 22 sandals on, at 7' 6½" inches tall Mohammad Alam Channa from Pakistan is also one of the world's tallest men.)

Glance down at your feet. They may not be the biggest in the world like Mr Channa's, but they're a remarkable and often neglected part of the human body. Humans have evolved over millions of years so that we can stand on feet. This may sound obvious, but it's an interesting and important fact. Other animals – like elephants or dogs – can only stand on their 'back legs' for a few seconds, and then usually have to fall back on to all fours. This ability to stand on our feet means we can move around and use our hands for more useful things than just getting about.

We also walk differently to most animals, which tend to walk on their toes. Our feet are long and broad and have to bear the whole weight of the body. We use our feet almost like springboards to launch into each stride.

Our toes are not like other animals either. Human toes are short and help balance the body. Monkeys have long flexible toes for gripping. Apes have a big toe which can grip in a similar way to our thumb and first finger. We can't do this with our feet. Our big toe lies alongside the other four. The muscles and bones of the legs and feet are much stronger than their equivalent in the arms. Early humans had long, powerful arms and rather stumpy legs. Much of our ancestors' time was spent swinging through forests that covered the earth. As these forests gradually disappeared, early humans found themselves having to travel greater distances in search of the good things in life. So legs became longer and more powerful. This was a great advantage over neighbours who had short legs, and longer-legged individuals did rather better at things like running away from enemies and hunting food. So it was they who survived, had children and began to evolve into us. (This is all part of Darwin's theory of evolution.)

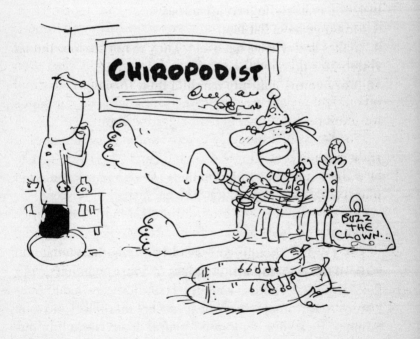

Ten Facts you may not know about your Feet.
1. 25% of the bones in the adult body are in the feet. Each foot has 26 bones.
2. The Achilles tendon at the back of the foot is the largest in the body. You use it to stand on your toes.
3. In your life you'll use your feet to walk about 50,000 miles.
4. The skin on the sole is the thickest on the body.
5. Everyone has fungus growing on their feet. If it gets out of hand – or out of foot – it's called athlete's foot.
6. No one knows why but right shoes tend to wear out faster than left ones.
7. In a few million years – if humans are still around – the little toe is likely to have disappeared.
8. Monkeys have flat feet.
9. Snakes and whales have feet. They're not obvious but all vertebrates do have them.
10. Very young children can bite their toenails.

Dear Dr Pete,
Did you know your right elbow is the one place you can't touch with your right hand?

Yes, I did. Although you should add the right wrist and most of the right forearm – unless of course you have very flexible joints! There is a medical condition (called Ehlers-Danlos Syndrome) where the joints are incredibly flexible. Some of these double-jointed people have worked in circuses as contortionists.

Did you know some of the other things you can't do – like hum with your nose closed, talk while you breathe in, and sneeze with your eyes open! Does anyone know any more?

Dear Dr Pete,
Can you change your smile? I smile like my brother, and I'd like to smile like a TV presenter.

The way that muscles of the face are used runs in families. So children often have smiles like their parents, brothers and sisters. We smile to show that we are pleased or amused. Babies smile first at about six weeks. They possibly learn to do this from their mums – a baby, even only just a month old – recognises that you smile at something good, or when you are happy. It is very difficult to change your smile and stay natural. Forced smiles look awful, and are easily recognised.

The muscles of the face have three basic movements. They can lower and raise your jaw to eat. They can move your lips to talk. And then they can move the face muscles to signal your mood.

The smile is a very complex action. What sort of smile you give depends on exactly how you feel. The smile when you are happy and relaxed at a party is very different from the more tight, nervous smirk you have when you are tense but feel you have to smile.

So what sort of smile is yours? All of us have these muscles arranged slightly differently. However, there are three basic types of smile.

Type One. This is the rather mysterious Mona Lisa smile. It has been described as smouldering. The corners of the mouth are pulled up and out by one particular muscle with a name almost longer than itself. This smile lasts between two and four seconds. It is often said to be the most genuine of the smiles because it uses muscles around the eyes – they 'smile' too – and it's not easy to fake.

Type Two. This is sometimes called a 'canine' or dog smile. The main movement is to raise the upper lip. It is often what we call a 'false' smile, and there is no use of the eyes. People who are nervous or trying to sell encyclopedias door-to-door tend to use this one.

Type Three. This is called the 'full denture' smile by the experts. Both sets of teeth are flashed as the muscles work together to pull the lips away from the teeth and pull the corners of the mouth out. This is the best smile to have if you want to advertise toothpaste or present TV programmes.

Look at a picture of yourself smiling, or go and practise quietly, looking in the bathroom mirror. Most people have a mixture of these three.

Which one are you? Whichever you are – even if you are not born to advertise toothpaste on TV for a living – remember it takes 43 muscles to frown and only 16 to smile. So save energy and smile!

Chapter 5
Intestines, Internal Organs and Digestion

Dear Dr Pete,
Why won't hospitals let you eat before an operation? I had
my appendix out recently.

You are not allowed to eat before an operation in which
you will need an anaesthetic to put you to sleep, because
the doctors want the stomach empty of food. If it were not,
the contents could spill over into the lungs during the
operation. Food in the lungs can produce a serious infection (pneumonia). You only have to go without food for a
few hours.

Dear Dr Pete,
Why doesn't your stomach digest itself?

Because it produces a thick mucus coat to protect itself. If a hole develops in this coating, then the strong stomach acid will make a hole in the stomach wall. It's called an ulcer.

This is a good question because if you think about it the stomach easily digests tripe. Tripe is the stomach of an animal such as a cow and is often eaten as food.

Dear Dr Pete,
Why don't you ever bite your tongue when you eat?

The tongue is a muscle, and its job is to taste food, to move the food around the mouth while it is being chewed and, with the lips, to form certain sounds of speech. (You use your tongue to say Dad, and your lips to say Mum! Try and see.)

The brain's control over these quite complicated acts, like chewing food and speaking, is brilliant. You can even do both more or less at the same time, if you want to. There is a risk of spitting some food out if you do, and this is one reason why it's thought to be rude to speak with your mouth full.

Anyway, the brain manages to send messages to co-ordinate all these actions and the result is that the tongue manages to keep out of the way of the teeth!

Dear Dr Pete,
Is it bad to swallow chewing gum? My younger sister swallowed some. Can it stick to your heart?

There isn't much point in swallowing chewing gum. These days it's basically an indigestible chewy man-made rubbery substance. In fact it's a by-product of the petroleum industry flavoured with sugar and one or two other things. (Years ago they made chewing gum from a natural rubber called chicle which was tapped from a South American tree.)

When you swallow a lump of gum it travels to the stomach. This is the widest part of the intestines, and there are no problems at all here. The next few yards (the small intestine) are quite narrow, and as the gum travels along mixing with food, there is a very slight danger, I suppose, of it lodging and blocking the whole system up.

The problem is not chewing gum's slight stickiness – jam is sticky and causes no problem – rather than that the gum stays in an indigestible lump, because it is not broken down by the digestive juices. If anything is going to get stuck it is usually right at the end of the narrow part of the small intestine. This is the point near the appendix where the small intestine joins the large intestine – often called the large bowel or colon.

I have never seen gum do this. However I've had patients who have been blocked off by orange segments which had been swallowed whole. Dried fruit and even a Brussels sprout have been known to cause the problem too.

So the lesson is to chew food well before you swallow it. There is certainly no need to worry about all this, as things will nearly always go right through you when you swallow them.

It is not true that chewing gum can damage the heart. Chewing gum will not stick to your heart if you swallow it. This odd belief began because people realised that the gullet – down which all food has to travel to get from the mouth to the stomach – does pass just behind the heart. So as you swallow your tea tonight it is less than a few centimetres behind the pumping heart.

However there is no fear of food sticking at this point. The gullet (oesophagus) is the most muscular part of the digestive tract and it will safely squeeze food by this area.

Dear Dr Pete,
Can you tell me why our waste matter is either brown or yellow?

The origin of the brown or yellow colour is in the red blood cells of the body. Blood is red because of the pigment haemoglobin – a substance contained in its red cells. Haemoglobin carries oxygen in the blood and it's a very complex substance whose structure was worked out in Cambridge in 1960. A simple description of it is that it's made up of iron (haem) and a protein (globin). The iron is obtained from food and the protein is made in the body.

There is a continual turnover of red blood cells. Each cell lasts about four months. This may seem a long time, but there are so many red cells that every second about two million have to be made to replace those lost. (It's about one million a second in children because their bodies are smaller and have less blood.)

This process makes for a lot of unwanted material that the body has to get rid of. Unlike household waste, which is collected once a week, waste from old, broken-down red cells is going out all the time. It travels out in bile. Bile is green and is made by the liver and stored in a little sac nearby called the gall bladder.

The gall bladder has a duct which passes to the alimentary tract. So the green bile can pass into the bowel, and then, with the waste of food substances not absorbed, it slowly travels to the toilet. This takes about one to two days.

When the bile starts this journey in the liver it is a green colour. As it journeys down the intestines, chemical changes happen and the pigments change to a yellow and then a more brown colour. If the journey is fast – as in diarrhoea or when the intestines are short – there is little time for all these changes and so the diarrhoea is usually yellow.

Food passes through a baby's intestine much faster than an adult' and it may be so quick as to make the diarrhoea green. Most mums have noticed this. Ask your mum if it ever happened to you.

You can see this whole process happen more easily as a bruise heals. When you hurt yourself blood may leak out into the tissues. If this blood is just under the skin it's called a bruise. A fresh bruise is dark blue-black because the haemoglobin in the blood loses its oxygen. As the days go by the bruise turns a green and yellow colour as pigments in the blood of the bruise change colour. These colour changes are very similar to the ones that take place in the intestines as the bile passes out of the body.

Dear Dr Pete,
Should you make someone sick if they swallow poison?

No. Get help fast. Try and find out for the doctor what has been swallowed, when it was swallowed and how much. The doctor MAY carefully make the patient sick later to get the poison up, but this isn't always done. Poisons like paraffin or petrol are best left in the stomach and diluted. If they are 'brought up', they could burn the gullet or spill over into the lungs and cause more damage.

Dear Dr Pete,
Is it true that the acid in the human stomach can burn a hole in a handkerchief?

The answer to that is yes. On the pH scale of acidity (0–14) 0 is very acidic and 14 very alkaline. (And 7 is neutral.) The hydrochloric acid (also called 'spirits of salts') of your stomach may have a pH as low as 1. This is quite able to burn a hole in a cotton handkerchief, if, for example, someone were to be sick into one and the acid were not washed away.

The inside of the stomach when this acid is present is undoubtedly the most acidic part of the body. The stomach wall protects itself from the corrosive nature of the acid by secreting and coating its wall with a special mucus. If this mucus fails to protect it an ulcer may result. If the acid happens to reflux up into the gullet where there is no protective mucus the pain is often known as heartburn.

PS. Just a note on acids. They have a sharp or sour taste, and turn litmus paper red. The first known acid was acetic acid. Vinegar is 3–6% acetic acid.

Dear Dr Pete,
If it is so cold in the Antarctic and everything freezes how do you go to the toilet? I wish I was an explorer.

I have been to the Antarctic twice – but I went at the easy time in the Antarctic summer. This is around our

Christmas. We were warm on our ship *Discovery*, and never had any trouble going to the toilet.

However, there can be problems in the Antarctic winter, when it can get down as low as minus 60°C. When it is very cold you can't just wee in the open. I met the explorer Robert Swann just after he had finished his walk to the South Pole. (He's since done a walk to the North Pole.) He told me that, in the really cold times, if you throw a glass of water into the air it will freeze before it hits the ground as ice. So you do have to find a sheltered toilet. This may be in one of the Antarctic base camps, or even a tent. When I was last in the Antarctic in 1985 the first over-wintering in tents had just been achieved.

The same protection from the weather is needed when you have your bowels open. You can't just squat down outside! Remember there is about 200 ml of water in what gets passed out when you empty your bowels. This could freeze, and be a very uncomfortable cause of constipation.

One true funny story: a doctor friend of mine, Denis, was living down in the Antarctic looking after the men in one of the bases. To pass the two years he was doing a study on the human body during times of extreme cold. He had some special body thermometers, and he persuaded his companions to swallow one each. These sent him radio messages of temperature readings as they passed through the men's bodies. As the men went about their day-to-day routine he knew what effect the cold was having on their inner temperatures.

The trouble was he only had a few of these special instruments. And they had to last the whole winter while the camp was cut off from the outside world. The toilet was an outside pit protected by just a tent. Occasionally the men forgot about the thermometers when they went to have their bowels open. Then my friend Denis would have to spend hours with a hammer and chisel chipping carefully away at piles of frozen poo!

I hope you become an explorer one day. It's a wonderful life. Beware of what work you do if you become a doctor or you could end up like my mate Denis. Or another doctor just back from the South Pole. His special interest to keep him busy was his friends' colds and runny noses in freezing conditions. His nickname became Snot of the Antarctic.

Why not admit it — you love your creature comforts...

Dear Dr Pete,
I have heard that you can die from eating liquorice.

HERE LIES A GENT FROM CREWE
WHO LIQUORICE LOVED TO CHEW.
HE WENT OVER THE TOP,
JUST COULD NOT STOP
AND AWAY HIS LIFE BLEW!

R.I.P.

This is true, if you eat huge amounts. Liquorice may cause a lowering of body potassium which can be dangerous.

I have read somewhere of a ship being wrecked on a beach. The ship was carrying liquorice and some of the locals plundered it and died after eating too much of the cargo. I can't check, as I can't remember where I read the story.

Liquorice is made from the long, sweet root of a plant. A black paste is extracted from this herb and can be made into sweets or into medicine. Liquorice contains two substances which can heal stomach ulcers.

This shows that all things are poisons. There is nothing harmless. Only the dose decides whether or not something is going to be a poison. (I didn't think of this clever statement. It was first said by a Swiss doctor called Paracelsus in the 1500s.)

Dear Dr Pete,
I have read that if you suck a lemon in the audience of a brass band then you can stop them playing?

If this trick works, it's only going to affect musical instruments that take a lot of blowing. (So no good for pianists). To play a brass or wind instrument you need a normal and steady control of saliva in your mouth. If your local trumpet player saw you sucking a lemon in the front row it could subconsciously make his or her mouth 'run'. You may find an increased flow of saliva just reading this and thinking about lemon juice which is a very potent stimulator of saliva from the six salivary glands set around the mouth. (Two under the jaw and one just under the ear on each side.)

After all this saliva has come into the mouth – that alone would make playing difficult – then the steady normal supply of saliva would tend to dry up for a short time while the salivary glands made some more. It is very difficult to play instruments like the trumpet or French horn with a dry mouth.

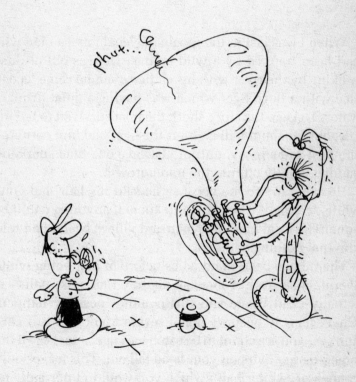

phut...

Chapter 6
Skin

Dear Dr Pete,
I heard you say on TV that you had seen a man whose hair
had gone white overnight. How does this happen?

When I was last in the jungle in Nepal I met a man who had been trapped by a wild animal. He was out at dusk walking by the river with his cattle, when he came face to face with a huge tiger which was having a quiet drink of water. To keep the story short, the man survived to tell his tale, but for about half an hour the tiger had him cornered amongst some rocks, until it just gave one final snarl and padded quietly off into the undergrowth.

He came to see me because he said his hair had gone white overnight. He wanted to know if anything could be done. The local medicine man and village healer had told him that nothing could be.

There have been many tales before of hair going white overnight because of shock. It doesn't. Hair – like nails – is actually dead tissue and this couldn't possibly happen. What seems to occur is that a severe fright – in this case thinking you are about to be eaten by a tiger – makes all the larger, darker hairs on your head fall out. This leaves only the lighter, whiter hairs which you wouldn't normally be able to see. The effect is to make it appear that the sufferer has gone 'white' overnight.

It actually takes about a week for this to happen, and when it does, it usually occurs about 3 months after the 'shock'. It was in fact about 3 months before I arrived in the remote village that the villager had stumbled on this tiger.

There are other cases in the history books of this happening. General Gordon's hair is said to have gone white during the siege of Khartoum, and Sir Thomas Moore's hair went white the night before his execution in 1535. One other case I have heard about was of a man imprisoned in the French penal colony of Devil's Island. He was due to be executed by having his head chopped off. There were several prisoners awaiting the guillotine and one morning at dawn he was trussed up and carried out to await the blade on his neck. Just as it was about to fall on him, the prison officer realised that they had brought the wrong person for that day's execution. So, the man was taken off the board to which they strapped the prisoners for the guillotine and taken back to his cell. Although he was later given a free pardon to try and make up for the mistake, it was said that his hair went white overnight and that he never spoke again.

Dear Dr Pete,
Can you tell me why people with eczema have:
a. constant goose pimples,
b. hands that turn bluish in cold weather,
c. and why if I run my nails along my forehead the marks remain for some time.

Eczema is an itchy, dry, red and scaly inflammation of the skin. It's often associated with allergy. The first thing to say is that not all people who have eczema will notice the things that you do. However, here are the explanations for the things that you write about:

a) True goose pimples are caused by very small muscles at the base of the hairs on your body. These muscles can erect the hairs in response to such things as cold and fear. That's why people talk about the hairs on the back of the neck standing up with fright. Some animals – like cats – can use these muscles to fluff up their coat when it's cold. This 'fluffed up' hair traps air around the body and helps keep the body warm. This is not really effective in humans because we have little body hair; the action is still retained, however, from when our ancestors were more hairy. There is no link between these true goose pimples and eczema.

However, the dry skin of eczema can sometimes feel rough and bumpy and similar to goose pimples because the hair follicle – the small hole from which each hair grows – becomes clogged up with keratin – the natural substance which makes up body hair. This is probably what you are feeling.

b) Some people with eczema are very susceptible to changes in the blood flow to the skin. In particular, the blood vessels to the skin of the hands and feet may become very narrow. This results in blood 'pooling' in the skin for longer than necessary. This blood tends to be blue rather than red because it has lost much of the oxygen. So the skin looks blue.

Eczema can also make the skin quite red and warm in other circumstances. It causes inflammation which can increase the blood flow to the skin. This red skin may make body temperature control in people with eczema quite difficult. The skin acts like a large radiator, and much body heat can be lost into the air.

c) Your final question, about your nails leaving marks on your forehead, is another interesting point. There is a link between eczema and a condition called white dermographism. In this white marks are left for quite a while after the skin is lightly scratched. You do not say if the marks are red or white. There is no link between eczema and a similar condition where the marks left are red. Are the marks red or white?

Dear Dr Pete,
I have got a very freckly nose, and I was wondering what to do about it. If I fell over, and skinned it right down the middle, when the skin grew back again, would it grow back without the freckles or with them?

The skin is made up of two layers called the dermis and epidermis. Between these two layers – rather like the jam in the middle of a sponge cake – is the strip of cells which is constantly forming the cells of the outer epidermis. The deeper layer is the dermis and it has within it, blood vessels, hair roots, sweat glands, and nerve endings.

Skin colour is determined by pigments which are found in the outer layer of the skin – the epidermis. Melanin is brown/black, and is the best known of these pigments. It's produced by cells called melanocytes in this outer layer. Carotene is the other skin pigment, and it's yellow/orange. (The pink colour of skin comes from small blood cells in the skin, and is not a pigment.)

Freckles are small brown flecks of skin colour, and they can appear in one of two ways. One sort of freckle is a collection of pigment in the outer layer of the skin. This 'freckle' tends to come out when sunlight falls on the skin. They are usually noticed in summer or abroad on holiday.

The other sort of 'freckle' is a collection of melanin-producing cells. These are a permanent fixture, and will not wear away like the first kind, which is really only a form of suntan. Freckles are commoner in fair-skinned people, and are especially common in redheads. As sunlight makes some freckles come out, you can use a sun block cream if you do not like them. Many people find them very attractive. Anyone who really does not like their freckles will have to camouflage them, as there is no way of getting rid of them.

If a graze strips off the outer layer of skin (painful!) this will destroy the melanin-producing cells and the skin will heal and be pale. I have a young patient aged 8 to whom this happened. However, these melanin cells have begun to appear again and the freckles are slowly coming back.

Deeper grazes – which damage the dermis layer of the skin – may cause scars and are not to be recommended to get rid of freckles.

Dear Dr Pete,
Where does the wax in ears come from?

Wax is made by the cells lining the ear canal. This is the passage from the outside world to the eardrum. Sound travels down here on its way to the brain. It's the part you can just get your little finger half-way down.

Wax is formed naturally in everyone's ear to protect the lining of this passage. Dust and dirt – and even some other funny things – get stuck in it, and then tiny brushes on the surface of the ear canal cells sweep this matter on to the bit called the pinna. That's the bit that sticks out of the side of your head.

Sometimes this wax can build up like a large boulder in a cave and block the entrance. If this happens you may not hear quite so well, but the wax can easily be washed out.

The best thing is to leave your ears alone, and let the wax clear naturally. Pins, little sticks with cotton wool on the ends, and the corners of towels can cause much greater problems than the wax. So one good rule is to never stick anything smaller than your elbow down your ear.

Dear Dr Pete,
We have a teacher with big, black, bushy eyebrows. What are eyebrows for?

Your teacher is a mammal. Mammals are animals which suckle their young and have body hair. In most of the 4,000 different species of mammals this hair coat is very useful to keep the body warm. Humans and a few other mammals have lost this coat, as it isn't really needed anymore. We have developed into animals who wear clothes, build homes, and know how to light fires. There are parts of the body where hair still grows, however. The hair on the head is the most obvious example, but there is hair under the arms and most of the body has some hair, even if it is so fine that you can't see it. (Palms and soles of the feet are two exceptions.)

The sex of a person determines patterns of adult body hair. Men tend to be hairier than women. This is mostly under the control of chemical messengers called the sex hormones. They control hair growth around puberty when the body changes to turn a 'child' into either the typical female or male shape and size.

One theory about hair differences between the sexes is that it makes recognition easier at distances. A beard, for example, indicates a man. Someone you might wish to meet with, or on the other hand to avoid if he looks fierce.

Some hairs have obvious uses. The fine hairs in the ear and nose protect against dust, dirt and insects. The eyelashes protect the eyes in a similar way. Your teacher's bushy eyebrows may stop sweat from the forehead running down into his eyes on a hot day or during a stressful lesson. Dark hair tends to be coarser than blond hair, and as men get older the eyebrows get longer and thicker. That's why your teacher's black eyebrows are thick and bushy. (I assume this teacher is a man!)

Dear Dr Pete,
You say mammals have hair. I've never seen a hairy whale!

What I said was that some mammals have lost this coat as it's not necessary for the lives that have evolved for them. If you look under the skin of a whale with a microscope you will find signs of where hairs once grew.

Chapter 7
Lungs and Breathing

Dear Dr Pete,
Why do doctors make you say '99' '99' when they listen to your chest?

This is a fairly old-fashioned – but very good – way of finding out if the lung in the chest is healthy. You place your stethoscope on the chest wall and ask the patient to say '99'. The sound heard gives a very good indication of the condition of the lung under the skin.

It is quite a skill to do this. Most doctors ask you twice because they move their stethoscope to the other lung to compare the sounds of the two sides. It's fairly easy to judge if these are the same – which they should be unless one lung is unhealthy.

Lungs get tapped by doctors' fingers for the same reason. Place a cloth over a heavy piece of wood and also a brick. Tap each lightly with your middle finger. The brick will sound stony and dull compared to the wood. A lung which contains water, because of an illness, will sound dull like the brick.

Dear Dr Pete,
Please could you tell me why and how we yawn. Is it a message from our body that we are tired, or is it something else?

Yawning is basically a deep breath in. It is a reflex action which means that it is something that happens automatically without your having to think about it. Even babies and animals yawn.

The purpose of a yawn seems to be to get more oxygen into the lungs. The body has decided that you need a boost – perhaps because you're tired. When you lose interest in something – maybe a boring lesson at school – your breathing tends to become less deep and effective. This clever reflex can put that right.

There is still a lot to learn about yawning. Why does it seem to be contagious? If one person in a group yawns why do the others quickly follow suit? This phenomenon has not been observed in animals, and the best explanation is that yawning is a way of letting other people close by know you are ready to sleep. This unspoken signal may be one way nature attempts to synchronise awake/sleep patterns amongst a group of people, and could have been useful for our ancestors, who didn't communicate with language as we know it.

If you were living together in a dwelling, such as a cave, it could obviously be useful if everyone went to sleep at the same time. It could be disruptive if some people were trying to get some sleep when other members were about to eat or go off hunting. It's a nice idea, even if there is no definite proof.

Dear Dr Pete,
What are the green things that collect up your nose?

These are a mixture of dust from the air breathed in, mucus secreted by the nose (better known as snot) and the bugs that live inside your nostrils. (These bugs – bacteria – can give the final product a green colour in case you've ever looked.) This mixture tends to dry out in the air stream passing through the nose and harden. They are often called bogeys. I don't know why.

It may be from the French word for imaginary person, or from a word which appeared in the last century meaning a hobgoblin, an evil spirit or bugbear. This is probably connected with the Scottish word bogle. Nobody knows for certain.

Dear Dr Pete,
Why can't you hum with your nose closed?

A hum is a low-pitched sound which comes from the vocal cords. The sound gets a characteristic resonance from the hollow bones (sinuses) of the face. You hum by breathing out through your nose with your mouth shut. If you pinch your nose the humming sound stops very soon because there is no way the air can get out. If you start humming and open your mouth, the sound changes. Try it. This isn't really the true low-pitched noise that we call a hum.

The sinuses are cavities within the skull, and they are extensions of the nasal space into the skull. The biggest is the maxillary sinus which is like a cave and takes up most of the space between the roots of the top teeth and floor of the eye socket. The sinuses act as resonators for the voice just as the wooden box of a violin does for its strings. There is no other known function, but they do reduce the weight of the skull which, if it were solid bone, would be a most unnecessary and difficult weight to live with.

I find all these things about the body fascinating. Can anyone tell me, for example, why we raise our eyebrows to sing a high note?

Dear Dr Pete,
Why do people hiccup, and what cure can you recommend?

A hiccup is basically a quick breath in. The air is drawn into the lungs by the flat muscle underneath the lungs called the diaphragm. However, unlike a normal breath when this action goes smoothly, the diaphragm 'twitches' and sucks air in quickly. As this happens the glottis – the entrance to the lungs at the back of the throat – snaps shut. This is what produces the hiccup sound. After this has happened the glottis opens and air is breathed out.

There are many causes of hiccups. Some are well understood. Others are not. Anything which 'irritates' the diaphragm muscle can produce hiccups. A common cause is to drink fizzy drink and then run around. The 'fizz' in the drink expands the stomach like a balloon and it presses up on the diaphragm.

There seems to be a hiccup centre in the brain too, and the impulse to hiccup can come from here. There are lots of 'cures' for hiccups. They range from breath holding – to break the rhythm of this pattern of breathing – to giving the hiccupping person a sudden shock by shouting. Other methods are pouring cold water down the back, a cold spoon down the back (usually preferred to the cold water), and drinking a glass of water from the far side of the glass.

Recently a doctor from Sussex, Philip Reading, has written to the doctors' paper the *Lancet* to say hiccups may be stopped if the victim sticks his or her fingers into the ears for about 20 seconds. It never fails, he says. The theory is that the fingers stimulate nerves carrying the hiccup feeling to the brain.

There isn't one certain cure. And, of course, most cases of hiccups do not have a serious cause and will disappear.

When you are resting, you breathe air in and out of your lungs about 12 times every minute.

Apart from breathing there are a number of interesting ways that air gets in and out of the lungs:

Yawning. A big breath in. One of the mysteries of yawning is why it is 'infectious' (see page 94). I bet since you began to read this paragraph about yawning many of you have either yawned or had to suppress one. (Not because this is boring you either!)

Speaking. Your voice is made by air passing out of the lungs past two vocal cords in your throat, which vibrate. You get a similar effect when you stretch an elastic band between your fingers. When you pluck it, it vibrates to produce a sound. You can experiment to show how your vocal cords work. Stretch the elastic band further for a higher sound.

Laughing. A laugh is a long breath out with some 'h' noises added in. Try it and see.

Coughing. A cough is a very quick blast of breath out.

Sneezing. A sneeze is like a cough but it is faster and goes out of the nose.

Snoring. A snore is the noise made when air is breathed in through both the nose and the mouth. This may cause the palate at the back of the throat to vibrate.

Dear Dr Pete,
I read your piece on cures for hiccups. I find that a teaspoon of vinegar works very well.

'Cures' for hiccups that have been recommened include drinking water out of the 'back' of a glass, peppermint water, holding your breath, and your remedy which is to drink a small amount of vinegar. There are a lot more. As I've said in the previous answer, a hiccup is a sudden breath in, followed by a sharp closure of the vocal cords in the throat. This is what makes the 'hic' sound. The usual cause, if there is an obvious one, is air in the stomach.

I don't think any of the 'cures' work reliably. If one of them did there wouldn't be so many to recommend. So I can't explain the vinegar drink. Most bouts of hiccups go just as suddenly as they came. If you have your own safe method that works for you stick with it, even if there's no clear explanation as to what's happening.

I say 'if your method is safe' because one man called John Mytton had heard that giving yourself a fright could be a cure for hiccups. So he set his pijamas alight and nearly died of burns.

The world record for hiccupping goes to Charles Osborne from the USA. He has been at it since 1922 (that's sixty-five years) and although he can't keep his false teeth in, he has still managed to marry twice and have eight children!

Chapter 8
Heart, Blood and Circulation

Dear Dr Pete,
My Dad goes to a health club and they take his pulse by
clipping something to his ear lobe. I didn't know the ear
lobe had a pulse?

The ear lobe has not got a pulse that *you* can feel, but modern electronic sensors can pick up one from this part of the body. A pulse is the 'thump' felt as blood is pumped from the heart through the arterial system of the circulation.

Doctors and first-aiders usually feel for the pulse of the heart at the wrist or the neck. The artery in the neck is about as thick as a finger, and the one at the wrist about the size of a pencil. So the 'thump' as blood passes by is easily felt with a finger placed over the right spot. The average resting pulse is about 70 beats per minute. Ear lobes have much smaller 'arteries'. In fact they are so small that they are given the name arterioles. There is no way that you could feel the pulse in one of these. These blood vessels are minute – you couldn't see one, never mind feel one. But they are there – that's why ear lobes are pink – and a sensitive electronic device can pick up the pulse as the heart thumps out each beat.

The ear lobe is a good place to clip your electronic device because it is out of the way, it doesn't hurt, and it will not easily fall off during vigorous exercise.

Keep fit enthusiasts carefully monitor their pulse rate for two reasons:

1. To monitor fitness. The pulse rate of a fit person at rest tends to be low, and to return to normal quickly after exercise.
2. To protect the heart from strain. To be safe, exercise should not put up the heart rate (pulse) more than a certain number of beats per minute. This varies a bit with age. If you are aged 15 this should not go above about 170 beats per minute. This is an 85% increase on the resting pulse. If you are young and healthy do not worry too much about your pulse rate during exercise. The body can take good care of itself.

A quick way to take your pulse during exercise is to count the rate over 6 seconds and then add a nought to that figure, that will give the number of beats per minute.

Dear Dr Pete,
Is the heart in the left side of the chest?

Despite the belief that the heart is on the left side of the human body, it is, in fact, about the size of your clenched fist and more or less in the centre of the chest. The most muscular of its four chambers is over towards the left side of the body, and so maybe this is where the idea comes from that the whole heart is on the left side. (Films which show firing squads aiming at a white handkerchief pinned over the left breast have no doubt added to the myth.)

This position of this muscular chamber is probably one reason why most mothers hold their babies with the child's head on the left side of their chest. Held like this the right ear of the baby is very close to the beating heart. (Before stethoscopes were invented doctors had to do a similar thing, and place their ear on the chest wall to listen to the heart.)

Newborn babies have just spent nearly nine months listening to their mother's heart beat in the warmth and security of the womb, and they find it a very comforting sound when birth launches them into a strange, cold world. Experiments have shown that babies will quickly settle and stop crying if they are played the sound of the heart.

Of course, nine out of ten mums are right-handed and so holding the baby like this leaves the right hand free to do things. But most left-handed mothers hold their baby in this position too. Watch out and see. It seems to be an instinctive thing.

Most mums do not realise why they hold their baby like this. You might like to ask a mum politely next time you see one with a new baby.

This may be why girls button their coats the other way around to boys. Most girls' clothes button up right side over the left. This is thought to be from centuries ago when women wore long cloaks. In this position they could bring the right arm and the right side of the garment over the baby held at the left breast.

(Men may button their coats and jackets up the other way round because years ago most held their weapons in their right hand. The left side of a cloak could be brought over the right hand. There were no pockets to put their hands in if it was cold, and the right hand could be kept warm without the risk of putting their sword down.)

Finally there is no need to fear that sleeping on your left side will damage the heart, or that injections should be given into the right arm – away from the heart. These are old wives' tales.

Dear Dr Pete,
How long does blood take to go around the body?

Blood leaves the heart with every pump of the heart. This happens about 70 times a minute with the body at rest. The time blood takes to go around the body – that is to say to return to the heart – varies according to where the blood is going. It takes about eight seconds to go up to the head and back. However, to get down the big toe and return to the chest may take nearly a minute.

When the blood returns to the heart after its journey, it needs to be replenished with oxygen from the lungs. It takes about six seconds to go to the lungs and then back again to the heart.

Blood doesn't flow at a constant speed. The fastest part of the journey is as it leaves the heart in the large artery called the aorta. When it gets to the minute capillaries, the red blood cells shuffle through these in single file. This is a much slower journey, it may take seconds to pass through a capillary, because these blood vessels are narrower than a human hair. Capillaries are responsible for the pink colour under your nails.

It has been worked out that if the blood from your body leaked out of a capillary it would take 100 years to fill a cup. This is because the vessels are so small only one red cell can pass out at a time. (There are 5 million red blood cells in a single pinprick of blood.)

There are many ways you can speed up the time blood takes to go round the body if you wish. The easiest way is to do some exercise. This can double the heart rate.

Dear Dr Pete,
Has the heart got anything to do with falling in love?

No. The brain is the seat of intellectual pursuits such as love and the other emotions. The first person that we know about to put this on record was Alcamaeon of Crotona. This was in 500 BC. Before that people believed the heart was the source of emotion. Another reason to link the heart and love is that the heart may speed up when we see – or perhaps even get close to someone we love – but the brain is behind all this. It is its nerves which speed up the heart.

Incidentally this man Alcamaeon, who was a pupil of Pythagoras, didn't get everything right. One of his ideas which has not stood the test of time was that goats breathed through their ears.

Dear Dr Pete,
Why can you hear the sound of the sea if you hold a shell to your ear?

You are hearing the sound of your own blood flowing inside your skull. It's called a 'venous hum' by doctors because it's the sound of the blood moving along your veins. Any shape similar to a shell will act as an echo chamber to enable you to hear this. And, of course, the shell shuts out other noises so that you can hear this very quiet sound.

Chapter 9
Miscellaneous

Dear Dr Pete,
Where do tears come from when you cry? If you cry a lot
does the water get used up? Why do tears taste salty?

Tears come from the two lacrimal glands. There is one above each eye. These produce lacrimal fluid (better known as tears). This fluid runs down a duct from the gland on to the surface of the eye. The tears then run across the eye and prevent it drying out.

You can always tell when he's taking his wife to see a weepy movie...

When you blink the upper eyelid acts like a windscreen wiper across the eye. You can't easily control blinking. It is a reflex action set off either by a dry eye surface or excessive tears – as produced in certain emotional states.

Tears don't normally spill out on to the cheeks because of the eyelid margins. These are 'greased' and made waterproof by glands in the eyelids which secrete an oily substance. So if excess tear fluid is produced the eyes will 'brim full of tears' before eventually running on to the face.

After the tear fluid has moved across the eye surface it drains away towards the inner part of the eye close to the nose. From here a duct takes it away into the inside of the nose, and that's usually the last seen of the 'tears'.

There is a very complex nerve supply to these tear glands above the eye. An increase in emotional tension stimulates these nerves, and they in turn make the lacrimal gland produce more tear fluid. This quickly drains to the eye – and this is best known as crying! These so-called 'emotional states' include happiness as well as sadness. People cry with joy. The body just registers the state of tension.

Yes, there is a limit to how much these glands can produce in one outburst, and tears will 'dry up' after a while – although there will still be enough to keep the eye from drying out.

At this stage the 'sad' emotional state is often called sobbing. Crying is associated with noises as well as tears. Sobbing is produced by a sharp intake of breath in compulsive or irresistible gasps.

Tears taste salty because they have got salt in them. Tear fluid is a very complex fluid. It's not unlike plasma, which is the watery part of blood without the red cells. It contains an enzyme – a substance known as lysozyme – which kills germs, and this helps protect the eye.

TOP TIP. If you get something like a piece of dust in your eye – rub the *other* eye. This will make both eyes water and will wash the dust out. If you rub the eye with the dust in there is a good chance you'll rub the dust further in and make the problem worse.

Dear Dr Pete,
My sister and I are identical twins. We look exactly alike and the teachers can not tell us apart. Would a blood-hound be able to smell any difference between us?

I just haven't got a clue...

The short answer is no. Many people will be surprised by this since human 'smell' is made up of so many different and complex things. However research shows that identical twins are so alike that a bloodhound can not tell them apart.

The bloodhound is the champion 'sniffer' amongst dogs. The area that detects smell inside the human nose is about 5 centimetres square. A sheepdog has 23 times as much as this, even though it is smaller than a human. Although the bloodhound is the champion dog at detecting smells, the overall world champion is the male Emperor moth. It can smell a new girlfriend 11 km (6.8 miles) away if the wind is in the right direction!

Dear Dr Pete,
Are witch doctors any good?

They may be. In many areas of the world there is no medical aid as you would expect in this country. There are no doctors who have been to university, there are no modern drugs, and no hospitals with things like X-rays.

In this situation there is often someone who takes the role of healer. He – it is usually a man – may be called a witch doctor or medicine man by us. This person usually has an extensive knowledge of drugs which are available from local herbs and plants. These often work very well indeed. He is often a very wise and experienced person whom the locals respect. So his advice is trusted. This trust – sometimes called bedside manner in the West – is a very powerful force for healing. If you believe in a person's ability to get you better then you may be half way to getting better.

The witch doctor may have other jobs. He may act as a priest. He may be involved in rituals to ensure good crops and plenty of rain if there is a drought. If someone disobeys him he may place a spell on that person. This is a very powerful sort of suggestion – as with the bedside manner – and that person may actually die if he or she believes in the spell.

Like all medicine men these people do not have all the answers. I had a witch doctor as a patient once. His own medicines hadn't helped a bad chest infection he had, and he rather reluctantly came to see me when he heard I was travelling in the jungle nearby. I managed to get him better with a course of penicillin, and once we knew that we respected one another, we became quite good friends. I learnt quite a lot from him before the expedition moved on.

Dear Dr Pete,
Why do men have nipples? I've got an extra one.

Men and women have bodies which are really quite similar. There are changes – mainly starting as you become a teenager – which cause the obvious differences. However, the hormones that do these work on a basically similar body. The ovaries in a woman are equivalent to a man's testicles. Even the penis of a boy has a counterpart in the girl – the clitoris.

In the woman, breasts have a function. That is to provide milk to feed a baby. In the male, this isn't necessary and the breasts – which are only modified sweat glands – do not develop. However as many as 50% of normal boys notice a slight swelling of one or both of the breasts as their hormones act during puberty. If you are wondering if this is happening to you, you can always go and check it out with your doctor. It's quite normal and makes the boy's nipple feel as if it has a Polo mint under the skin.

Many people – boys and girls – have extra nipples down the front of the body. These are a throwback to the human body's evolution. A lot of animals have more than two nipples. These are needed by, for example, cats and dogs, because they will usually have many more than one to feed in their litter.

There are other parts of our bodies which are vestigial. (This means they are leftover signs from previous times but are not now necessary to normal life). The appendix is one. In animals which feed on grass this part of the bowel is much longer and is necessary to break this food down.

Incidentally, although nowadays having an extra nipple

does not cause problems, this has not always been the case. In medieval times women with extra nipples were suspected of being witches, and using these to suckle the devil!

Dear Dr Pete,
My Grandad has two artificial hips. Will he be able to go through customs, or will he set off their detectors?

Yes, your grandad will set off the metal detectors at Customs. These are designed to pick out people carrying guns. I have spoken to HM Customs and they say that this sort of thing is quite common, and all he needs to do is to explain about his metal hip replacements.

What he will get – so Customs tell me – is a quick 'rub down'. Sounds fun! The Customs officer will feel over his body with the flat of his hand. He won't have to take any clothes off, but will be searched to check that he hasn't got a gun on him.

Customs tell me there are quite a lot of unnecessary worries about things like this. Diabetics who need insulin injections often wonder if they will be suspected of being drug addicts because they're carrying a syringe. All you have to do is explain.

A few months ago I flew back to London from Nepal and went through 'Nothing to Declare', but was stopped and searched. They found a plastic container on me with used – and bloody – syringes, plus a quantity of morphine. It's difficult to think of more suspicious circumstances, and I felt I was in for a hard time.

However, I explained that I was a doctor and had needed the drugs on an expedition. I said I was bringing the used needles, etc. home as there was nowhere to dispose of them safely in the villages I'd been travelling through. They knew I was telling the truth and simply waved me through.

Dear Dr Pete,
If you take paracetamol (which seems to work for most pains) how does it know which part of your body to cure?

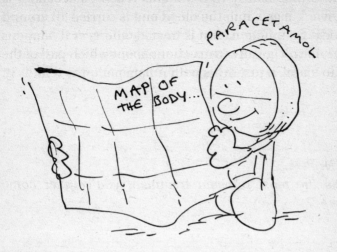

You might think that such a commonly-used drug as paracetamol would have a simple way of working. This is not the case. (If you are under 12 you may well have taken paracetamol for something like earache without realising it. This is because the drug is sold under names such as Calpol and Disprol.)

Aspirin is another drug with a similar action. It isn't used now in the under 12s because it may very, very rarely cause problems in young people.

Paracetamol works against inflammation in the body.

Pain + swelling + hotness and redness = inflammation.

There are a lot of complex body chemicals involved in this equation, and paracetamol works to counter them. So it reduces inflammation, and along with that the pain involved. (As well as the redness, swelling and hotness or temperature.)

It does this mainly in the brain. When paracetamol is swallowed, it gets into the blood and is carried all around the body. So inflammation is treated wherever it happens to be. It hasn't got any instructions about which part of the body to 'cure', it just deals with inflammation as it finds it.

Dear Dr Pete,
What's the most unusual treatment you've ever come across?

The cannonball treatment. I read about it in one of the top American medical journals of 1 August 1896.

A 3–4 pound cannonball was recommended for the treatment of constipation. The patient lay on his or her back and the writer warned that the use of the heavy iron ball should be 'thorough and systematic'.

The sufferer was advised to roll the ball over the surface of the belly for five to ten minutes morning and night. The 'treatment' should end by the ball being balanced on the belly button for a few minutes.

I asked a famous bowel specialist if this would have done any good – or harm! He thought it might have worked by the weight of the ball breaking up the hard matter in the bowel and stimulating the muscles in the bowel to move the remnants of food down to the rectum and then out of the body down the toilet.

I've tried it out once with a 3 pound pirates' cannonball from the Indian Ocean. It seemed to work. The next day my patient had diarrhoea. But I'm not convinced that it was the cannonball at work, as she had eaten a shellfish curry the day before.

Dear Dr Pete,
There is an expression 'dead weight'. Is the human body heavier after death than in life?

No. The weight is the same. After death – or when unconscious – the body is relaxed and this makes it more difficult to handle as it flops about. In life the muscles are under a natural tension, and this makes the body easier to handle, and may make it seem lighter.

Hundreds of years ago, some experiments were done to find the weight of a person's soul. The body was weighed just before (this must have been rather alarming!) and just after death. The weight readings were the same.

Dear Dr Pete,
Why do my fingers go wrinkly if I spend time in the bath?

Your skin wrinkles up in the bath because of the keratin in the outer layer (epidermis) of your skin. This protein substance swells when it absorbs water, and as this epidermis is fixed to the layer underneath it, this has the effect of throwing the skin into folds and wrinkles. You'll notice this on your hands and feet because this is where the outer layer of skin is thickest – places on the body where the thicker skin protects you from wear and tear.

Dear Dr Pete,
My friend has been told by her doctor that she has a rare and serious disease called HAGS. This is supposed to be very catching. She asked the doctor could anything be done. He said yes, they must lock my friend in her bedroom, throw away the key, and then feed her kippers. Will kippers cure HAGS? yours sincerely, Worried of Wimbledon.

Dear Worried of Wimbledon, No. Kippers will not cure "HAGS". There's no cure. It's just that kippers are the only food you can get under the door, regards Doctor Pete.

P.S. For serious readers there is no such disease as "HAGS". I take it "Worried of Wimbledon" that you are having me on!

120

Rolf Harris

YOUR CARTOON TIME

Did you know that you can draw?

Rolf Harris shows you how – clearly and
simply – in *Your Cartoon Time*.
Starting with stick figures, he explains how to
develop these step-by-step into your own
stylish characters, and there are ideas too for
how you can use your drawings – as birthday
cards, home movies and so on.

Drawing is fun!

All you need is a pencil, paper and Rolf
Harris's book – *Your Cartoon Time*.

Another Knight Book

Michael Johnstone

YOUR NUMBER'S UP

Do you know what the seven deadly sins are?
And the seven colours of the rainbow? And do
you know why the arithmetic book was so
upset? It was full of problems . . .

Countless braincrunching quizzes, numerous
fascinating number facts and multiple
mindless jokes in a mesmerising mathematical
miscellany.

Carol Gold and Hugh Westrup of the Ontario Science Centre

THE SPORTS BOOK
The Science of Sport

What does science have to do with sport? Lots. It explains how balls travel through the air, how drag slows down athletes and how sports equipment has changed over the years. It tells how muscles work when you run and jump, why world records are always being broken and how your brain and body type affect your performance.

A lively and informative look at the science behind sports using facts and easy to perform experiments.

Marian Hardless

WHIZZ QUIZ

Why were cowboys often buried in their boots?
a because it was supposed to bring them luck
   in the next world
b because they were usually worn out and
   therefore no use to anyone else
c because they were stuck to their feet

Are you a whizz at quizzes?
Do you know what the word for chocolate
means?
Or how to work out what height a child will
grow to?
Or why dinosaurs laid small eggs?

WHIZZ QUIZ has the answers – and the
questions too!